The Essential Guide

Written by Hannah Dolan

CONTENTS

INTRODUCTION

Believe it or not, you are in the presence of greatness. An ancient prophecy says that one day, a Special one will unite the people of the world. He or she will lead them into battle against a powerful man who wants to plunge the world into a permanent, unchanging eternity so that no one can ever mess it up with weird stuff. Who will be the hero of the biggest, most important, most epic saga of all time?

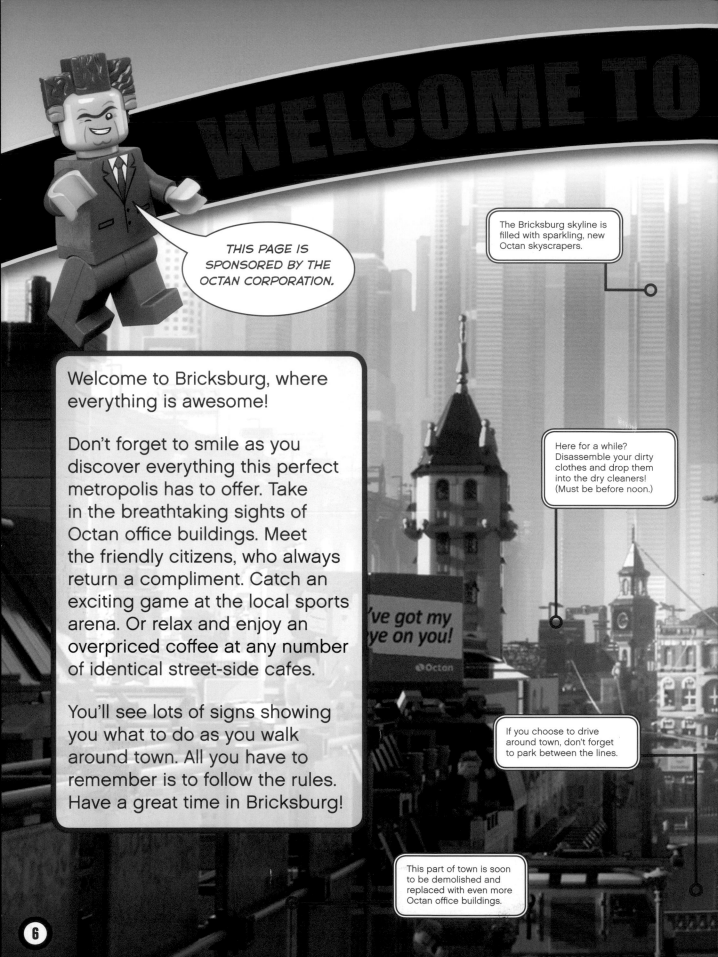

WELCOME TO

THIS PAGE IS SPONSORED BY THE OCTAN CORPORATION.

Welcome to Bricksburg, where everything is awesome!

Don't forget to smile as you discover everything this perfect metropolis has to offer. Take in the breathtaking sights of Octan office buildings. Meet the friendly citizens, who always return a compliment. Catch an exciting game at the local sports arena. Or relax and enjoy an overpriced coffee at any number of identical street-side cafes.

You'll see lots of signs showing you what to do as you walk around town. All you have to remember is to follow the rules. Have a great time in Bricksburg!

The Bricksburg skyline is filled with sparkling, new Octan skyscrapers.

Here for a while? Disassemble your dirty clothes and drop them into the dry cleaners! (Must be before noon.)

've got my ye on you!

Octan

If you choose to drive around town, don't forget to park between the lines.

This part of town is soon to be demolished and replaced with even more Octan office buildings.

WE'RE BUILDING A BETTER BRICKSBURG.

"Grab an overpriced coffee from me for only $37!"

Larry the Barista

The Bricksburg monorail service is always on time.

"Eat at the sports bar. Their chicken wings are delicious!"

Frank the Foreman

This is the symbol of the Octan Corporation, which is owned by President Business, the leader of Bricksburg.

"The surf's great here, brah."

Surfer Dave

"Stop by and say hello to my cats. There's Fluffy, Fluffy Jr, Fluffy Sr..."

Mrs Scratchen-Post

EMMET

Meet Emmet, the most ordinary guy in Bricksburg. No one, not even Emmet himself, thinks there's anything special about him. But all that changes when Emmet accidentally finds a mysterious object. From that day on, he becomes the greatest, most important person in the universe – honest!

Instructions For Life
Emmet always follows the steps in his instructions manual, which was written by President Business. It tells him how to be a model Bricksburg citizen.

EVERYTHING IS AWESOME!

Emmet blends in on the building site in his bright orange overalls.

Did You Know?
Construction workers like Emmet are some of the most commonly found minifigures in real-world LEGO® City-themed sets.

Always Be Happy
Emmet always has a happy face because he loves his life in Bricksburg. He loves his job as a construction worker. He loves following President Business's rules and instructions, and never, ever questions them. He also loves chicken wings and croissants.

Emmet's... Favourite Things

Favourite Song:
Let's see! It's got to be "Everything is Awesome". I could sing it for hours, and hours, and hours...

Favourite TV show:
Where Are My Pants?, of course!

Favourite restaurant:
Any chain restaurant.

Construction Worker

Emmet works at Bricksburg's construction site as part of a busy crew of builders. He does such a good job of fitting in that none of his colleagues remembers much about him. He's just another smiling, yellow face in the crowd.

Dramatic Day

What starts off as an ordinary day takes a dramatic turn when Emmet falls down a hole at the construction site. He later finds himself inside a scary Melting Room, with a strange object stuck to his back – and it seems someone wants to melt it off him! Emmet is soon to discover that he has found the powerful Piece of Resistance, and that makes him a pretty extraordinary guy.

Laser beam, about to melt the Piece of Resistance off Emmet.

The Piece of Resistance is now permanently stuck to Emmet's back.

WHAT IS THIS THING ON MY BACK!?

This lever adjusts the laser machine so it's perfectly positioned to zap its target.

Chained to the Melting Room chair, there's no escape for Emmet!

A DAY IN THE LIFE OF EMMET

Bricksburg citizens like Emmet begin each day by consulting *How To Fit In, Have Everyone Like You and Always Be Happy*. This book of instructions contains step-by-step diagrams that show the citizens exactly how to live, so they never, ever have to think for themselves.

After greeting the walls, door, ceiling and floor of his home, Emmet takes his book of instructions from the bookshelf and begins to follow his instructions for the day...

1 Breathe in and then out. Make sure you do it in the correct order!

2 Greet the day, smile and say "Good morning, city!"

3

Exercise. How about jumping jacks?
Hit 'em – one, two, three...

4

Shower, shave your face, brush your teeth
and comb your hair smooth.

5

Wear clothes. Remember to assemble the
right ones for your job!

6

Watch TV with all the special people,
or houseplants, in your life.

7

Greet your neighbours. Say "hello" to Mrs
Scratchen-Post and "meow" to her cats.

8

Purchase an overpriced coffee on your way
to work. Another awesome day has begun!

WYLDSTYLE

Wyldstyle is a free spirit who hates following President Business's rules. A highly skilled, streetwise Master Builder, she can build anything out of anything. When Wyldstyle discovers the Special who is destined to save the world, she vows to do all she can to help him fulfill his destiny – even if it is a rules-follower like Emmet!

> WE NEED TO BUILD OUR WAY OUT OF HERE!

Wyld By Name
Wyldstyle might look mean and moody, but beneath her black hood, Wyldstyle isn't quite as tough as you might think. Deep down, she can be a little insecure – that's why she often changes her name to sound cooler! She was known as Darkstorm, Gemini and then Snazzypants before she became Wyldstyle.

A graffiti tag makes Wyldstyle's tracksuit look even cooler (if that's possible).

Encountering Emmet
Wyldstyle first meets Emmet at the Bricksburg construction site. She is there looking for the Piece of Resistance – a powerful object that, according to an ancient prophecy, will one day be found by the greatest Master Builder of all time. Unfortunately for Wyldstyle, Emmet accidentally finds it first!

Wyldstyle uses a grappling hook when she needs to escape the authorities.

Wyldstyle's... Guide To Master Building

Keep it secret.
You must keep everything I say here confidential. The Master Builders are a secret, underground society of creative builders who refuse to follow President Business's rules.

Use anything.
Master Builders build with anything and everything we can see around us.

There are no rules.
Don't let anyone tell you what to build. Master Builders make up their own instructions for building anything they like.

IS THAT YOUR REAL NAME?

LET'S **NOT** TALK ABOUT MY NAME.

Building Bravery
When Wyldstyle rescues Emmet from the Melting Room, he discovers just how daring she is. He is even more impressed when she builds an awesome motorcycle out of junk – but he wishes she'd stick to the speed limit!

Hazard sign tells the police to steer clear of this deadly dragster.

If this motorcycle wasn't cool enough already, it also has flames!

WHAT'S ON IN

This is your guide to another great week of television in Bricksburg, brought to you by the Octan Corporation. Follow President Business's instructions by tuning in to fit in with all the other rules-following citizens of Bricksburg. Have a great week, everybody!

Where Are My Pants?

7pm Daily

Will this guy finally find his pants this week? Of course not!

Now on its seven-thousandth episode, this smash-hit sitcom just keeps getting better. Meet a regular guy who just wants to find his pants, but no one seems to know where they are! Be sure to tune in for more pants-searching pandemonium.

Is that an unusual vase behind *Where Are My Pants?* guy's wife, or is it his pants?

4/5 Bricks

  Winner of 3 Octan TV Awards

BRICKSBURG

Party on down with President Business!

Don't Miss This!

Taco Tuesday

6pm Tuesday
Party On, Little People!

Tune in from 6pm for a live broadcast from Octan Tower, where President Business will be holding a loud and lively Taco Tuesday fiesta party. Join in and dance like there's no tomorrow!

5/5 Bricks

"Hola, I'll see you on Tuesday!"
Taco Tuesday Man

Take A Taco
Next Tuesday, there'll be only one question on everyone's lips: WHO WANTS A TACO?! Every rules-following citizen should gather on the streets to receive a free taco from Taco Tuesday Man.

LORD BUSINESS

This is one cool guy! At least, everyone in Bricksburg thinks so. In public, he is President Business, who makes Bricksburg the awesome place it is. But President Business isn't all he seems – there is also a scary side to him. Make way for Mr Big Boy Pants, Lord Business!

President Business

In exchange for free tacos and his love, all President Business asks of his minifigure citizens is that they follow his instructions very carefully, so everything in Bricksburg is just perfect. (Otherwise they will be put to sleep.)

Leader, Hero, Director...

President Business likes to control everything in Bricksburg. When he thinks his staff aren't directing the TV show *Where Are My Pants?* to his high standards, he steps in and takes over.

Horns double as coffee cups for when he needs a pick-me-up.

At the push of a button, this red light comes on to make him appear even scarier.

Lord Business's... Guide To Being A Good Boss

Control everything.
If you want something done well, you might as well do it yourself.

Know that you are always right.
Never listen to anyone else's ideas. Yours are the best.

Dress snappily.
To be the part, you have to look the part. No one messes with anyone who is wearing stilt boots and shoulder pads.

The Kragle
This is Lord Business's super weapon. It has the power to glue the world, so everything can stay just the way Lord Business likes it – forever. Only one thing can stop the Kragle: the legendary Piece of Resistance.

I MEAN BUSINESS!

Leg stilts allow Lord Business to tower over everyone.

Lord Business

Behind closed doors, President Business transforms into who he really is inside: Lord Business. No more Mr Nice Guy, Lord Business has a plan for world domination. He will use the Kragle to end the world – and it will happen on Taco Tuesday!

OCTAN TOWER

A mega-sized company like the Octan Corporation needs a mega-sized office building. The imposing Octan Tower is the base from which Lord Business and his staff of robot minions control every product, company and citizen in Bricksburg and beyond.

> HOW SCARY CAN SOMEONE'S OFFICE BE?

Relic Room

Way up on the infinitieth floor of the Octan Tower is Lord Business's Relic Room. It is where Lord Business displays his collection of strange and dangerous objects from another world, all of which can entrap, snap and zap any unwelcome visitors! Lord Business's most prized relic is the Kragle.

High Security

All visitors must have their security passes ready for inspection by Velma Staplebot. Lord Business's overbearing personal assistant prevents any unauthorised persons from entering his private office.

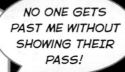

NO ONE GETS PAST ME WITHOUT SHOWING THEIR PASS!

OCTAN TOWER
SECURITY PASS
ROBOT

Did You Know?

Lord Business has a huge staff of robots at his command. Nine kinds of robot minifigures can be found inside the various *LEGO Movie*-themed sets.

Octan Studios

The TV show *Where Are My Pants?* is broadcast from inside Octan Tower. Lord Business instructs his staff to make sure it is mindless enough for his citizens. He wants it to brainwash them so they lose their creativity, and never question his rules.

BAD COP/ GOOD COP

Bad Cop/Good Cop is Lord Business's number one henchman. At least, the bad side of his split personality is. Now that there are rumours that the Special is on the loose with the Piece of Resistance, Lord Business has no time for Good Cop's brand of polite policing.

Helmet worn mostly for protection around Lord Business.

Approachable smile makes everyone feel more comfortable.

Ma and Pa Cop
Policing runs in the family. Bad Cop/Good Cop's parents are small-town cops. He finds himself in a bind when Lord Business orders him to freeze them with the Kragle. Will his good side or his bad side win out?

POLICED TO MEET YOU!

Police radio, used to say a friendly "hello" to fellow officers.

Good Cop
Meet your friendly neighbourhood police officer! Need a croissant or a glass of water whilst being interrogated? It's Good Cop you want to talk to. Good Cop prefers to kill crime with kindness.

Catching sight of these flashing lights strikes fear in Master Builders.

Door flips up when Bad Cop wants to unleash the cop car's laser cannons.

Spoiler makes the cop car aerodynamic so it can reach huge speeds.

POLICE

SUPER SECRET

Cop Car

When Bad Cop is in the driving seat, this bad-boy police car can outrun almost any vehicle a Master Builder can assemble. Good Cop prefers to enjoy coffee and doughnuts in it.

Dual laser cannons take down Master Builders at a distance.

Sunglasses, worn to intimidate Master Builders, and to look cool.

HE'S WANTED: BROKEN OR ASSEMBLED!

Bad Cop's... Mission

1. Capture the Special.
Find the Special one from the Prophecy, who has the Piece of Resistance.

2. Find the Master Builders.
Discover the hiding places of every single underground Master Builder.

3. Restore law and order.
Lord Business's rules are the law. They must be adhered to.

Bricksburg police badge marks him out as an authority figure.

Bad Cop

When Lord Business has dirty work to do, he calls on Bad Cop. His latest assignment is to catch the Special, and if Bad Cop doesn't do the job, Lord Business definitely won't show him HIS good side!

OTHER WORLDS

There are many worlds beyond Bricksburg – you just have to know where to look! Minifigures were once free to roam between worlds and share ideas. But Lord Business didn't like it, so he had walls built between the different realms. Now, only Master Builders can travel between worlds via secret tunnels.

Did You Know?
Other distant lands in *The LEGO Movie* world include Pirate's Cove, Viking's Landing and Clown Town.

The Old West

Welcome to the land of cowboys and cavalry, covered wagons and cacti. As you explore the Old West's frontier town, you might want to prepare for a showdown at high noon.... There's a suspicious-looking sheriff on horseback and he appears to be expecting trouble!

When this bell rings, it's high noon. Time to draw!

Calamity Drone spies for Lord Business whilst can-can dancing.

Rootbeer Belle's cold drinks are dynamite on a hot day.

YEAH, THIS PLACE LOOKS PRETTY GREAT, BUT WE HAVE A TERRIBLE LEECH PROBLEM.

Middle Zealand

This wondrous realm of forests and waterfalls is home to many brave knights. Here, you will find castles, mutton... oh, and DRAGONS! That could be why Emmet and Wyldstyle only pass through here when they're on the run from Bad Cop.

Wanted: The Special

There's an ordinary-looking minifigure wanted in this town, and Bad Cop's here to find him. Emmet and Wyldstyle are here looking for someone, too: the wise Master Builder who prophesied the Special.

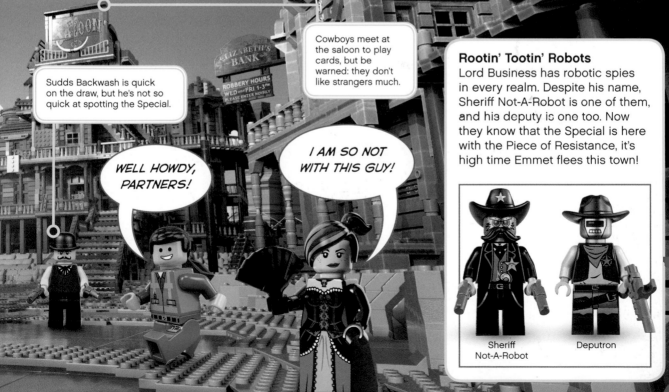

Cowboys meet at the saloon to play cards, but be warned: they don't like strangers much.

Sudds Backwash is quick on the draw, but he's not so quick at spotting the Special.

Rootin' Tootin' Robots

Lord Business has robotic spies in every realm. Despite his name, Sheriff Not-A-Robot is one of them, and his deputy is one too. Now they know that the Special is here with the Piece of Resistance, it's high time Emmet flees this town!

WELL HOWDY, PARTNERS!

I AM SO NOT WITH THIS GUY!

Sheriff Not-A-Robot

Deputron

VITRUVIUS

This ancient, Master Building wizard remembers life before everyone was forced to follow rules. Vitruvius is the one who foresaw that a Special will one day find the Piece of Resistance, and use it to stop Lord Business from ending the world with the Kragle – but Lord Business thinks that is hippy dippy baloney!

Only a Master Building wizard could look good in a sparkly cape.

Vitruvius's sense of style is far out, man.

Blinding Beam

Not all that long ago, Vitruvius could see, and he also had the Kragle. Lord Business blinded him with a laser beam in order to seize the powerful weapon.

Wise Wizard

This blind wizard doesn't need the power of sight to be an ace Master Builder. He can see the instructions in his mind. Vitruvius doesn't need his eyes to see that Emmet is the Special, either.

Old West Hideout
Since his showdown with Lord Business, Vitruvius has been hiding out as a piano player in an Old West saloon. When Emmet and Wyldstyle find him, he invites them back to his apartment, which Vitruvius has decorated in his own, unusual style!

BUILD FROM YOUR HEART!

Vitruvius thinks his glowing staff is magical, but it looks a lot like a chewed-up lollipop!

Did You Know?
Vitruvius is the first real-world LEGO minifigure ever to wear a sparkly cape.

Vitruvius's... Tips For New Master Builders

Be observant.
Use your surroundings for building inspiration.

Visualise your build.
See it in your mind. I find meditation helps.

Believe in yourself.
Trust your instincts. Unless your instincts are terrible.

The Special
When Vitruvius first presents Emmet to his fellow Master Builders as the Special from his Prophecy, they boo and jeer Emmet – but Vitruvius still believes in him. He teaches Emmet that if he trusts in himself, he will become the greatest Master Builder of all.

THE PROPHECY

UHH... YES, THAT'S ME.

Emmet certainly has a face of yellow, but it's not particularly special.

These hands haven't created anything original – ever!

When Lord Business seized the Kragle, he thought nothing could stop him ending the world with it. But Vitruvius foresaw one last hope: the Special. If the Special could find the legendary Piece of Resistance and fit it onto the Kragle, he or she would stop the Kragle from releasing its power. Since Emmet found the Piece, he must be the Special of Vitruvius's Prophecy. But Emmet isn't quite what everyone expected!

Did you know?

The population of minifigures in the world is three times that of China. Can you believe that Emmet is the most special one of all

Emmet didn't exactly find the Piece of Resistance. Rather, it found him when it became stuck to his back. Emmet didn't like it much!

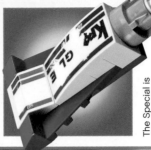

The Special is supposed to have some great ideas for thwarting the Kragle, but Emmet hasn't had an original idea in his life!

THE PROPHECY

One day, a talented lass or fellow...

A Special One with face of yellow...

Will make the Piece of Resistance found...

From its hiding refuge underground...

And with a noble army at the helm...

This Master Builder will thwart the Kragle and save the realm...

And be the greatest, most interesting, most important person of all times...

All this is true because it rhymes.

Wyldstyle spotted Emmet with the Piece of Resistance stuck to his back and realised he was the Special. Now, she (and soon, a rag-tag bunch of Master Builders) is behind him, whether she likes it or not!

BATMAN

As if Batman didn't have enough amazing talents, he is also a brilliant Master Builder! He likes to think of himself as pretty special, but when the actual Special from Vitruvius's Prophecy needs his help, he's there – even if he thinks Emmet is a disappointing ding-dong.

> I ONLY WORK IN BLACK, AND SOMETIMES VERY, VERY DARK GREY.

All awesome super heroes need an emblem. Batman's is the bat-symbol.

A black cape completes Batman's dark and brooding look.

The Dark Knight

Heroes don't come much cooler than this caped crusader. By night, Batman builds and fights crime in his all-black Batsuit. By day, Batman dons a super-slick business suit to become his alter-ego: Bruce Wayne, CEO of Wayne Enterprises.

A bat-eared mask hides Batman's real identity, and gives off an edgy, mysterious air.

Bat Builds

Batman likes to build bat-themed vehicles, like the Batwing he rescues Emmet, Wyldstyle and Vitruvius in. He has fitted out his Batwing with subwoofers that blast out the bass on his awesome tunes – very, very loudly!

Batarang, for hitting short-range targets (always on the first try).

Did You Know?

Since he first appeared in minifigure form in 2006, Batman has worn 13 different Batsuits – but they have always been in black or shades of grey.

THIS IS A SONG I WROTE FOR WYLDSTYLE. IT'S ABOUT HOW I'M AN ORPHAN.

Batman's... Guide To Being Cool

Be tall.
The ears on my Batsuit make me several millimetres taller.

Be dark.
I only wear black, and sometimes very, very dark grey.

Be mysterious.
I achieve this by leading a double life: as Batman, and as my alter-ego, Bruce Wayne.

Brooding Boyfriend

Batman is in a relationship with Wyldstyle, but it's not super serious. He expresses his love by penning dark and brooding love songs for her, but they're mostly about his first love: himself!

HERE IN CLOUD CUCKOO LAND, THERE ARE NO RULES!

Head for the big bright thing in the sky and follow the rainbow: that's how to find the secret realm of Cloud Cuckoo Land, the most creative place in the universe. It is home to weird and wonderful creatures, and things that just don't make sense. Imaginations can run free here, because there are no limits or rules of any kind.

Crazy Creations

Anything goes in this playful paradise! The architecture doesn't follow the same rules and regulations that Emmet is used to in Bricksburg. The buildings are all crazily different sizes and shapes. The whole realm is built on top of a cloud, so making things stable doesn't matter much here anyway!

The sun always shines in Cloud Cuckoo Land.

Bright flowers bring any building to life.

MY EDGY GRAFFITI TAG WOULD BE WASTED ON THIS BUILDING.

There are no signs telling you what to do here. The residents prefer psychedelic swirls.

Up here, there are plenty of fluffy clouds to use for decoration.

WHEN THERE ARE NO RULES, I AM ALWAYS ON TIME!

CUCKOO LAND

These swirling steps could lead somewhere, or nowhere. It doesn't matter here!

Buildings can look like anything here, from a whale beached on a cloud to an enormous eye.

Building in many colours is the Cloud Cuckoo Land way.

THIS PLACE IS WAY TOO CUCKOO FOR ME.

The Dog
A land with no limits or rules is the perfect place for a creative bunch of Master Builders to meet. Vitruvius gathers them all at the Dog, a strange and silly secret meeting place shaped like a puppy. He has a 'Special' announcement to make.

ASSEMBLE THE MASTER BUILDERS!

When Lord Business came to power, he banned all creativity. He ordered Bad Cop to hunt down Master Builders, and those who weren't captured were forced into hiding. Now that the Special has arisen, the time has come for the remaining Master Builders to unite against Lord Business.

Did You Know?

The Master Builders are from all walks of life. Some are from the LEGO Minifigures Collectibles line, some are licensed characters and some were created for The LEGO Movie.

BAD COP'S FILE OF MASTER BUILDERS AT LARGE

Super Heroes

Superman

Building style:
Possesses out-of-this world, super-minifigure building powers.

Additional file notes:
Finds Green Lantern extremely irritating.

Super Heroes

Green Lantern

Building style:
Can build almost anything out of thin air using a special, super-powered ring.

Additional file notes:
Likes to be near Superman.

Super Heroes

Wonder Woman

Building style:
Uses her lasso of truth to grab building materials at incredible speeds.

Additional file notes:
Occasionally forgets where she parked her invisible jet.

Super Heroes

Johnny Thunder

Building style:
An expert in building for survival in the wilderness.

Additional file notes:
No hiding place is too dangerous or remote for this adventurer.

Super Heroes

Green Ninja

Building style:
Whips up a building whirlwind using his golden kantana swords.

Additional file notes:
A master of stealth, he can be hard to catch.

Historical Figures

William Shakespeare

Building style:
Thinks all the world's a stage. He builds entire scenes.

Additional file notes:
Writes about his building creations.

Historical Figures

Forestman

Building style:
Steals bricks from the rich and builds for the poor.

Additional file notes:
Is rarely seen without his band of merry men.

Historical Figures

Egyptian Queen

Building style:
Builds like an Egyptian.

Additional file notes:
Her pet snake can be vicious. Even she is a little scared of it!

Creative Types

Magician

Building style:
With a wave of his wand, he can assemble builds with an added element of surprise.

Additional file notes:
If approached, he does a disappearing act.

Creative Types

Artist

Building style:
Creating Master Building masterpieces with artistic flair.

Additional file notes:
Never spotted without his beret and paint splashes.

Creative Types

Circus Clown

Building style:
Humorous builds with inbuilt gags and a bold colour scheme.

Additional file notes:
No one knows what he looks like underneath his makeup.

Everyday Heroes

Hazmat Guy

Building style:
Building with materials used to store hazardous waste.

Additional file notes:
Do not approach without protective clothing.

UNIKITTY

It's impossible to be unhappy around this delightful Master Builder! Hailing from Cloud Cuckoo Land, the land of rainbows, puppies and absolutely NO negativity, Unikitty likes to look on the brighter side of life.

Unikitty would call this colour a sunny sky blue.

ANY IDEA IS A GOOD IDEA... EXCEPT THE NOT HAPPY ONES!

Unikitty is as colourful as her homeland.

Sweet Self

This half-unicorn, half-kitten welcomes everyone to Cloud Cuckoo Land with a dance and a smile! Unikitty only likes to think of positive things. If she ever starts to feel the opposite of happiness, she thinks of bubble gum, butterflies and candy floss to make the thoughts go away.

Happy Building

Unikitty is a Master Builder who loves to build cute, rainbow-coloured, sparkly things. Even weapons can be happy-looking. This cannon fires pretty flowers at Unikitty's enemies.

Master Of Disguise

Unikitty changes according to her situation. When she needs to be professional, she's Biznis Kitty. In space, she's Astro Kitty. Unfortunately for her, on the high seas, she becomes Queasy Kitty!

Watch out for this flower cannonball if you have hayfever!

Unikitty's... Not Happy Things

Rules, bedtimes, babysitters, governments, furballs, dark colors, frowny faces, instructions, bushy moustaches and rainy days.

Did You Know?

Always dressed for the occasion, Unikitty appears in five different guises in *The LEGO Movie*-themed sets.

No one wants to be looked at with these narrowed eyes!

MESS WITH THE CAT, YOU GET THE HORNS!

Angry Kitty

When Lord Business's robots attack her home and her Master Builder friends, Unikitty loses control of her positive thoughts. She becomes scary-looking Angry Kitty. Watch out, Lord Business!

Biznis Kitty

Astro Kitty

Queasy Kitty

LORD BUSINESS'S ROBOT ARMY

What's the best way to get everything done just the way you like it? Build your own robot army to do it for you! There must be a jillion robots under Lord Business's command, all programmed to do specific jobs to his exacting standards.

ROBOTS, DESTROY THE SPECIAL!

All Executrons work in sharp, black suits to show that they mean business.

Executron
Executrons are some of Lord Business's most trusted robotic staff. They work behind the scenes to ensure his evil schemes run efficiently.

Skeletron
Skeletrons are the backbone of Lord Business's security staff. They guard Lord Business's private office to ensure the Kragle is safe and secure.

Bad Cop Boss
All robot police teams work directly under Bad Cop. When Lord Business has concerns that the good side of his henchman is getting in the way of his evil plans, he literally erases that side of his face. Now, Bad Cop can carry out Lord Business's dirty work with a clean conscience.

Every Micro Manager looks different, but they all have long arms to grab minifigures with.

Micro Managers
Lord Business expects total perfection from his Micro Management team, and they deliver. When he unleashes his super weapon on the world, these Micro Managers force Bricksburg citizens into the perfect positions that they will be frozen in forever.

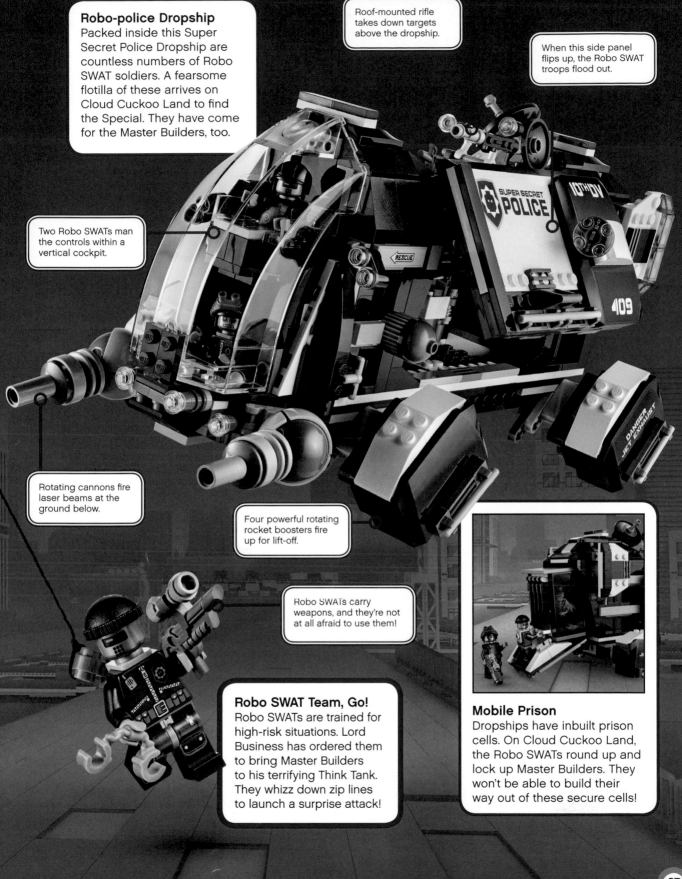

Robo-police Dropship
Packed inside this Super Secret Police Dropship are countless numbers of Robo SWAT soldiers. A fearsome flotilla of these arrives on Cloud Cuckoo Land to find the Special. They have come for the Master Builders, too.

Roof-mounted rifle takes down targets above the dropship.

When this side panel flips up, the Robo SWAT troops flood out.

Two Robo SWATs man the controls within a vertical cockpit.

Rotating cannons fire laser beams at the ground below.

Four powerful rotating rocket boosters fire up for lift-off.

Robo SWATs carry weapons, and they're not at all afraid to use them!

Robo SWAT Team, Go!
Robo SWATs are trained for high-risk situations. Lord Business has ordered them to bring Master Builders to his terrifying Think Tank. They whizz down zip lines to launch a surprise attack!

Mobile Prison
Dropships have inbuilt prison cells. On Cloud Cuckoo Land, the Robo SWATs round up and lock up Master Builders. They won't be able to build their way out of these secure cells!

WHAT KIND OF BUILDER ARE YOU?

All of the Master Builders are extremely talented and imaginative when it comes to building, but they each have their own ideas and style, too. Even Emmet has some ideas of his own, though they're not always entirely helpful. Which Master Builder are you most like?

Save Our Submarine
Can you tell which builder assembled each part of this wacky-looking watercraft? When Lord Business's robots launch a surprise attack on Cloud Cuckoo Land, the Master Builders work together to build this submarine and escape underwater.

Do you prefer to build with bright colours instead of muted tones?

NO

YES

Could your builds be described as dark and edgy?

YES

NO

NO

Do your builds contain natural shapes and features?

NO

YES

Are all your building ideas happy ones?

YES

38

Do you have a passion for bats? **YES** →

You're Batman
Batman only ever builds in his trademark black and grey tones. He also likes to build things in his own, bat-shaped image.

no

Do you adore retro things? **no** →

You're Wyldstyle
Wyldstyle has an urban building style, which looks even edgier when she adds her own graffiti tags.

YES

no

You're Vitruvius
Vitruvius gets back to nature when he builds, using natural, earthy colours. He usually adds dream-catchers in case he needs to take a nap.

Do you think building a double-decker couch is a good idea? **YES** →

You're Emmet
Emmet's style is niche and, some would say, impractical. His one idea is a double-decker couch, so all his friends can watch TV together!

no

Are you obsessed with spaceships? **YES** →

You're Unikitty
Rainbows, sparkles and extremely bright colours are the hallmarks of a Unikitty build.

You're Benny
Benny prefers to build classic 1980s-era spaceships. At rare times when he can't, he always builds in the same retro style.

BENNY

His fellow Master Builders know him as 1980-something space guy. His friends know him as Benny. But there's one thing everybody knows about this classic spaceman: he loves spaceships, spaceships, **spaceships!**

Retro Logo
The logo on Benny's spacesuit shows that he helped to fly the first fleet of classic LEGO spaceships in the 1980s. Benny thinks everything was better in the eighties – especially spaceships.

Oxygen tank for breathing in space, worn by Benny at all times.

Zero Gravity
Gravity doesn't apply to Benny. When he meets with his fellow Master Builders at Cloud Cuckoo Land, Benny finds it hard not to float out of place.

Racing To Space
Space hero Benny is always ready to take one giant leap for minifigure kind in his retro blue spacesuit. He has been wearing it since the 1980s – no wonder his helmet looks a little battle-scarred!

Benny's...
Retro Pastimes

1. Playing games on reel-to-reel punch card computers.

2. Listening to music on cassette tapes.

3. Watching space adventure movies using a video recorder.

If you look closely, you might spot moondust on Benny's spacesuit! Or is it just plain old dirt?

Spaceship!

Benny thinks all problems, big or small, can be solved by building a spaceship – and he's usually right. He is over the moon when he finally gets the chance to build the coolest spaceship ever to fight back against Lord Business and his robot army.

SPACESHIP! SPACESHIP! SPACESHIP!

Benny finds his happy place when he's in outer space.

Did You Know?

Classic Blue Spaceman minifigures like Benny were released in real-world LEGO sets from 1984 to1988.

Benny must be feeling a little light-headed. The crack in his helmet has made his oxygen supply leak out.

THE THINK TANK

In the heart of Octan Tower is a terrifying chamber known as the Think Tank. It is the final part of Lord Business's plan to control the world. The many thousands of Master Builders who have been captured by Lord Business's forces have been brought here to have their creativity zapped out of them.

Sinister Cells
The Master Builders' heads are attached to brain-sucking machines, which extract their ideas and creativity against their will.

NO! WHOA! AHHHHH!

Thousands of Master Builders are securely strapped into endless rows of cells, with no hope of escape.

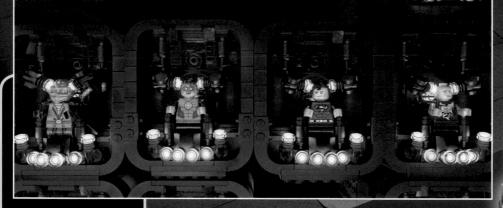

Neighbours
Just when Superman thinks things couldn't get any worse, he finds himself loaded into the cell next door to Green Lantern, who he finds incredibly irritating!

Powerful Ideas
The Master Builders' ideas create the instructions to build anything in the world. Now, Lord Business wants to make the ultimate set of instructions, for the Kraglizer: a huge cube that will unleash the power of the Kragle all over the world. He won't ask politely for their ideas to help him do it!

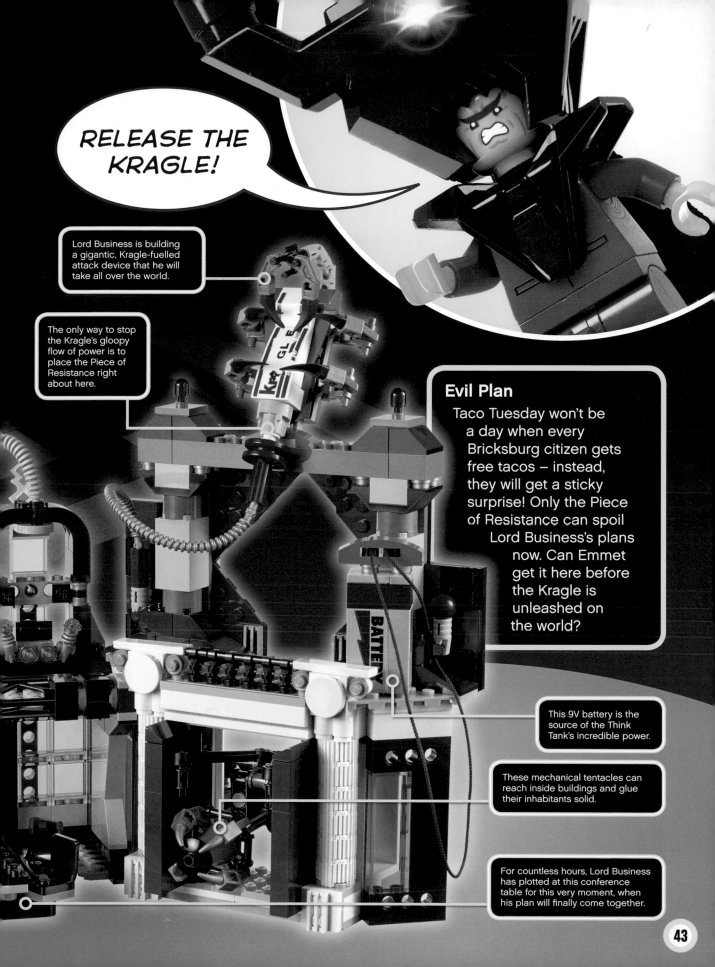

RELEASE THE KRAGLE!

Lord Business is building a gigantic, Kragle-fuelled attack device that he will take all over the world.

The only way to stop the Kragle's gloopy flow of power is to place the Piece of Resistance right about here.

Evil Plan

Taco Tuesday won't be a day when every Bricksburg citizen gets free tacos – instead, they will get a sticky surprise! Only the Piece of Resistance can spoil Lord Business's plans now. Can Emmet get it here before the Kragle is unleashed on the world?

This 9V battery is the source of the Think Tank's incredible power.

These mechanical tentacles can reach inside buildings and glue their inhabitants solid.

For countless hours, Lord Business has plotted at this conference table for this very moment, when his plan will finally come together.

EMMET VS BATMAN
LOVE MATCH

At first glance, this might not look like a fair match. No one wants to be compared to the Dark Knight! But Emmet has fallen head over heels for Wyldstyle, and now she must choose between Emmet and her current boyfriend, Batman. Who will win her heart?

Knight in Shining Armour

Emmet has already fallen for Wyldstyle by the time he discovers she has a boyfriend who, unfortunately for Emmet, happens to heroically rescue them from certain death. Great!

Real Romance

When strong, independent Wyldstyle first meets Emmet, she thinks he's nothing special, just a regular, rules-following guy. But she soon sees that they're not all that different. Emmet can see the real person behind her tough girl act, whose name isn't really Wyldstyle – it's Lucy!

EMMET

Height: 51 mm

Attractiveness: 7.
His instructions tell him to be well groomed.

Strength: 7.
He lifts pretty heavy bricks at the construction site.

Popularity: 2.
Emmet does such a good job of fitting in that no one notices him.

Teamwork: 9.
He knows it's important to work together to achieve great things.

Master Building: 1.
His one attempt was the double-decker couch. Enough said!

Coolness: 2.
He's the opposite of cool.

Creativity: 6.
He has some great ideas. He just needs to believe he has them.

Romance: 9.
Emmet would do anything for the one he loves.

Happiness: 9.
He is happy in all he does, whether he's following instructions or being creative.

Big Ideas: 1

BATMAN

Height: 53 mm
(In his bat-mask.)

Attractiveness: 8.
His heroic look is hard to resist.

Strength: 9.
Fighting bad guys part-time requires supreme physical fitness.

Popularity: 9.
The world over loves Batman.

Teamwork: 2.
Batman works alone, and he doesn't like to share bricks.

Master Building: 9.
He builds like he fights crime. Very well indeed!

Coolness: 10.
He's Batman, for goodness sake!

Creativity: 6.
He sometimes steals Emmet's ideas and claims them as his own.

Romance: 3.
He's a little too self-centred to be a great boyfriend.

Happiness: 2.
His tragic childhood makes him a dark and brooding soul.

Big Ideas: 0

METALBEARD

This here pirate has witnessed many strange and dramatic events on the high seas, but no story is as great as that of the fabled Special. MetalBeard is a stubborn barnacle about Emmet to begin with, but he soon realises that if the Master Builders get behind him as a hearty crew, they will defeat Lord Business once and for all.

AVAST MATEYS, I HAVE RETURNED!

MetalBeard keeps his pet shark at arm's length.

Grasping fingers made from pieces of a ship's hull.

MetalBeard's pet parrot could squawk a thousand tales.

Telescope, for spotting Micro Managers at long range.

Revenge, Mateys!
MetalBeard has waited a long time to reap revenge on Lord Business and his robot army. The last time they met, he was lucky to escape with his head. It was a massacre too terrible to speak of... except he tells the grisly tale at every opportunity!

The Sea Cow
There's no mistaking MetalBeard's crazy-looking ship when she sails over the horizon. The Sea Cow is a welcome sight when the Master Builders are lost at sea on Emmet's double-decker couch, after their submarine breaks into pieces.

Pirate hat emblazoned with a minifigure skull and wrench bones.

Pirate Machine

MetalBeard still rues the day he was forced to use his building skills to replace his strapping pirate body with a hodgepodge of pirate-ship parts. On the plus side, he is now the Swiss army knife of pirates. What pirate wouldn't want a cannon for an arm?

Why have one cannon when you can have two? And a spare steering wheel to boot.

MetalBeard's... Guide To Pirate Speak

1. Begin every sentence with "Arr" to get the attention of yer hearty crew.

2. Refer to yer shipmates as "Mateys".

3. It be wise to use the word "be" in place of "is".

MetalBeard stores all the organs he has left inside this aptly placed treasure chest.

Who needs matching feet? MetalBeard's body is functional, but definitely not fancy!

MetalBeard even has a built-in leg holster for his pirate pistol.

MetalBeard

If you take away his pirate-part body, not much of the original MetalBeard remains. He has only his vital organs, his head and, luckily, his signature metal beard.

EMMET'S BIG IDEA

Emmet realises that if the Master Builders work together as a team and follow instructions, just like he does in his job at the construction site, they can achieve great things. This is "Emmet's Plan to Get Inside the Tower, Put the Piece of Resistance on the Kragle and Save the World".

I CAN GET US ANYWHERE!

1. Emmet has assembled many buildings using instructions, but no one would expect the Master Builders to follow instructions!

2. Emmet gets the gang to work together and follow instructions to build a spaceship. It looks exactly like all the other delivery ships arriving at Octan Tower.

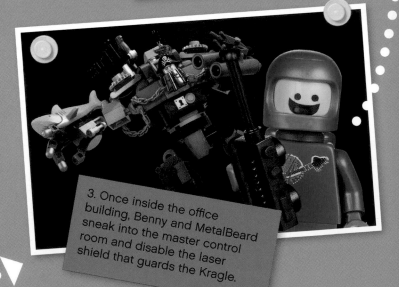

3. Once inside the office building, Benny and MetalBeard sneak into the master control room and disable the laser shield that guards the Kragle.

4. Vitruvius provides lookout. He makes sure Benny and MetalBeard are not being followed by Lord Business's robots.

5. In slick business-like disguises, Unikitty and Batman (as Bruce Wayne) enter Lord Business's boardroom. They persuade him to make one last change to the Kraglizer in order to stall its release on the world.

6. Next, Wyldstyle and Emmet sneak into the Kragle Room disguised as robots. They place the Piece of Resistance on the Kragle.

And save the World!!

7. They all save the world. Easy peasy!

EVERYTHING IS AWESOME"

Minifigures all over the world love to bop to the beat of the catchy tune "Everything is Awesome". It's been top of the pop charts for as long as anyone can remember. On the way to work, during work, when you're trying to break into Lord Business's office – any time is a great time to sing it!

OH MY GOSH, I LOVE THIS SONG!

Closet Fan
Wyldstyle prefers the deep and dark 'real' music Batman writes to this cheesy pop tune. But when Emmet forces Wyldstyle to sing it in order to fit in with Lord Business's robots, she joins in and, strangely, seems to know all the words!

JOIN IN AND FIT IN, EVERYBODY!

Everything is Awesome!
Everything is cool
when you're part of a team.
Everything is awesome
when you're living a dream!
Turn that frown upside down,
Let's see your smiles all around.
Everything is Awesome!
Everything is cool
when you are part of a team.
Everything is awesome
when you're living a dream!
Everything is better
when we stick together,
Side by side, you and I are gonna win forever.
Let's party forever!
We're the same, I'm like you, you're like me,
We all work in harmony!
Everything is Awesome!
Everything is cool
when you're part of a team.
Everything is awesome
when you're living our dream!

BUILD YOUR OWN WAY

Even if you're not the Special, if you believe you are capable of anything – and the world depends on it – you can be the most talented, most interesting and most extraordinary person in the universe. Emmet's big idea doesn't stop the Kragle, but just trying it out is enough to make the Master Builders see that anyone can be special.

Follow The Instructions

When rules-followers like the citizens of Bricksburg make a plan and work together to achieve it, they can do amazing things. Emmet knows that sometimes following rules can be a good thing. The instructions he makes for his "Plan to Get Inside the Tower…" even look a lot like those Lord Business gives out to his citizens.

Ghost Vitruvius

Vitruvius never made it out of Octan Tower. He died. But he has returned as Ghost Vitruvius! As a ghost, he tells Emmet that he made up the Prophecy. He did it to prove that the only thing anyone needs to be the Special is to believe that you can be.

Inspiring Leader

With her newfound knowledge that everyone is special if they believe they can be, Wyldstyle comes up with a new plan to save the world – but the Master Builders can't do it alone. She storms Octan Studios and broadcasts a message to the citizens of Bricksburg: if they all put their ideas together, they can build an army of ideas to save them all!

Imagine Ideas

All on their own, Master Builders can use their creativity to build anything out of anything. If it weren't for Master Builders like Unikitty and Wyldstyle, the world wouldn't exist. But they can learn something from rules-followers like Emmet, too: if they all work together, they can save the world!

WORKING TOGETHER IS A HAPPY IDEA!

BREAKING THE RULES

The citizens of Bricksburg used to be happy to follow President Business's instructions, but hearing Wyldstyle's inspiring words has made them realise that, just like the Master Builders, they have their own great building ideas, too. They disassemble their everyday vehicles and transform them into combat ships, built for battle against Lord Business.

What was once a giant cone sign is now a giant cone gun!

Minifigures can hear the ice cream van's music for miles around thanks to these speakers.

These ice lolly missiles could knock a Micro Manager out cold!

What flavour ice cream would you like? You can choose from this flavours board.

Ice Cream Machine

Ice Cream Mike and Ice Cream Jo usually serve the citizens icy treats, but their van is now a chilling flying machine. When Lord Business sees it, he will get his just desserts!

Trash Chomper

Garbage Man Grant's garbage truck keeps the city streets clean. Its rear loader has transformed into a mashing mouth, ready to clear up Lord Business's Micro Managers!

Wings feature cannons to do damage, and a broom for cleaning up afterwards!

Scary snapping jaws, poised to trash a Micro Manager.

This part of the truck can hold gigantic amounts of tiny garbage.

Octan ● RUBBISH

G 349

RP 70805

Wing water-sprayers can be turned on and off like a tap.

Toilet seat target finder helps Joe to aim his cannon at menacing machines.

Plumber Joe is equipped for any job, big or small, thanks to all these tools.

Octan's
JOE'S
PLUMBING

JOE'S PLUMBING

Flying Flusher

Plumber Joe zips around town in his plumbing van to help minifigures with leaky bricks. Now, he's flushing away Lord Business's forces in his powerful plumbing plane!

BATTLE OF THE BUILDS

Taco Tuesday has arrived, but there are no free tacos in sight. Instead, the citizens of Bricksburg are about to get Kragled! Armed with ideas and their new creative contraptions, do the citizens have the power to overcome their sticky situation? They battle for their lives against Lord Business's menacing machines!

Hank Hayseed has turned his Old West windmill into a helicopter. Its chicken lookout tells him where to drop his carrot bombs!

Bricksburg Builds

As more and more Bricksburg citizens begin to realise that they can use their ideas to fight back against Lord Business's forces, a formidable fleet of creative craft rises up to join the battle.

Kabob Bob has transformed his popular kabob stand into a meaty mean machine. Watch out for its condiment squirters!

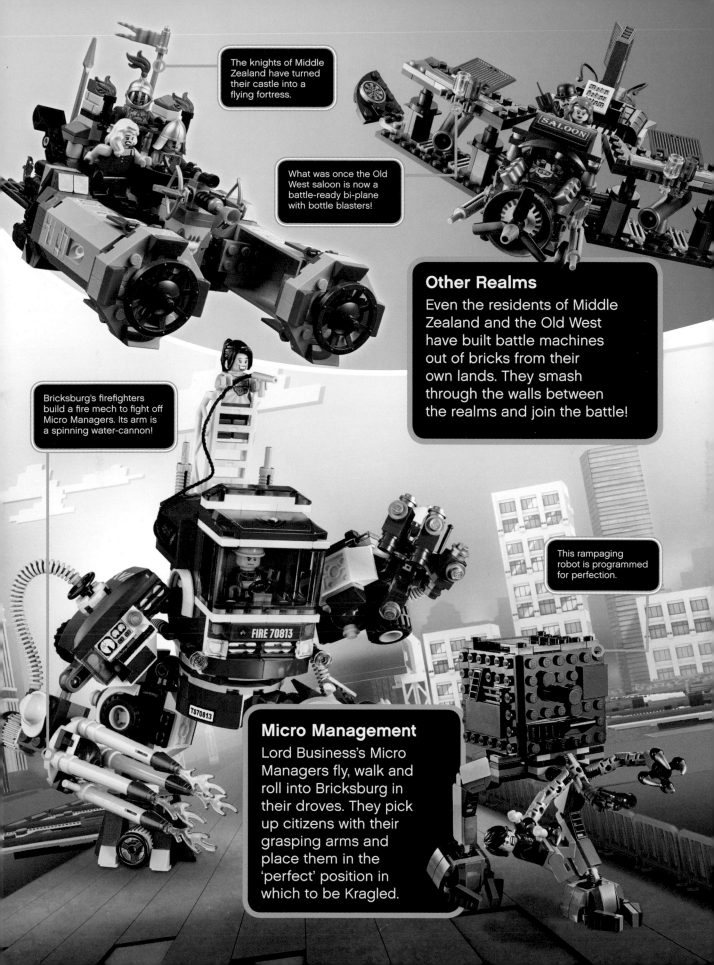

The knights of Middle Zealand have turned their castle into a flying fortress.

What was once the Old West saloon is now a battle-ready bi-plane with bottle blasters!

Other Realms

Even the residents of Middle Zealand and the Old West have built battle machines out of bricks from their own lands. They smash through the walls between the realms and join the battle!

Bricksburg's firefighters build a fire mech to fight off Micro Managers. Its arm is a spinning water-cannon!

This rampaging robot is programmed for perfection.

FIRE 70813

TS70813

Micro Management

Lord Business's Micro Managers fly, walk and roll into Bricksburg in their droves. They pick up citizens with their grasping arms and place them in the 'perfect' position in which to be Kragled.

SALOON

TO THE KRAGLIZER!

A huge street and air battle rages on in Bricksburg, but the Kraglizer is still spraying its gloopy glue all over the city. It's time to stop it – and Lord Business's plans for world domination – once and for all! The Master Builders assemble a building plan that will turn Taco Tuesday into Freedom Friday, except it'll still be a Tuesday.

These engines pack enough power to smash through the walls between the realms.

A blue-suited spaceman needs a blue spaceship, with coordinating wing fins.

Benny's Spaceship
If the coolest classic spaceship of all time can't reach the Kraglizer, nothing can! Benny finally gets a chance to build his favourite kind of spaceship. A space-suited Wyldstyle and Astro Kitty are also on board as they dogfight their way past robot units to reach the Kraglizer.

Satellite dish for communication with Master Builders on the ground.

No one can fly this spaceship like Benny can!

SPACESHIP! SPACESHIP! **SPACESHIP!**

Aerodynamic nose helps this ship whizz past Micro Managers.

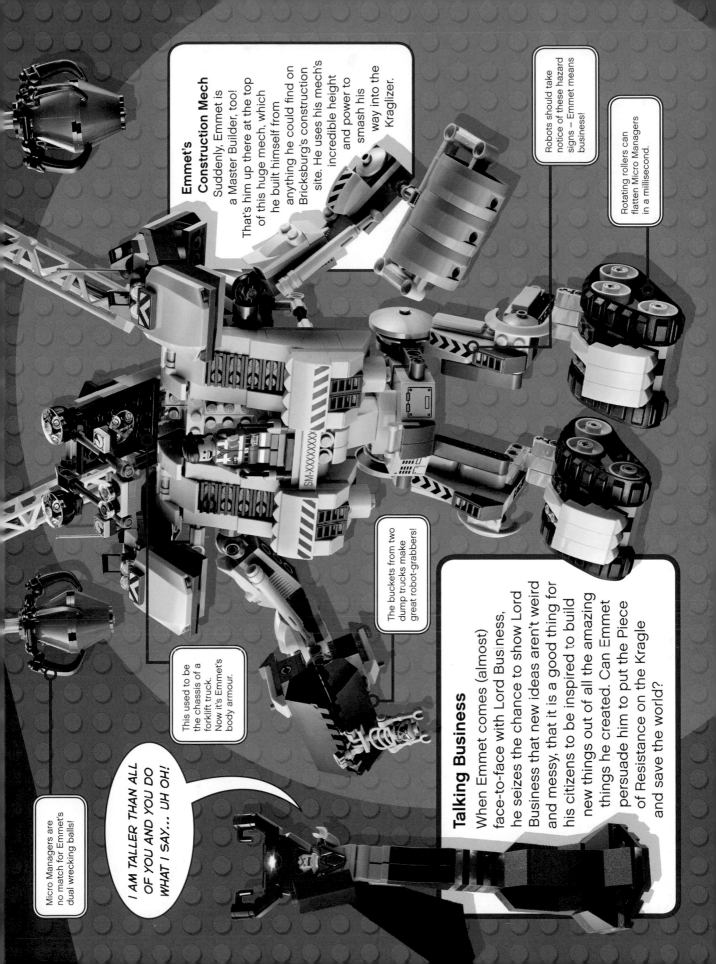

Emmet's Construction Mech

Suddenly, Emmet is a Master Builder, too! That's him up there at the top of this huge mech, which he built himself from anything he could find on Bricksburg's construction site. He uses his mech's incredible height and power to smash his way into the Kraglizer.

Robots should take notice of these hazard signs – Emmet means business!

Rotating rollers can flatten Micro Managers in a millisecond.

The buckets from two dump trucks make great robot-grabbers!

Talking Business

When Emmet comes (almost) face-to-face with Lord Business, he seizes the chance to show Lord Business that new ideas aren't weird and messy, that it is a good thing for his citizens to be inspired to build new things out of all the amazing things he created. Can Emmet persuade him to put the Piece of Resistance on the Kragle and save the world?

This used to be the chassis of a forklift truck. Now it's Emmet's body armour.

Micro Managers are no match for Emmet's dual wrecking balls!

I AM TALLER THAN ALL OF YOU AND YOU DO WHAT I SAY... UH OH!

SM-XXXXXXXX

BUILDING A BETTER

This rag-tag bunch have gone and saved the world! They are all proof that anyone can be the most talented, most important, most extraordinary person in the universe if you just believe you can do amazing things. Now that the gang don't have a world to save – or control, in Lord Business's case – where are they now?

Realising the error of his ways, Bad Cop found his good side again and scribbled on a homemade happy face where it used to be. Only Good Cop patrols Bricksburg now, handing out doughnuts wherever he goes.

8:00

Benny is still as passionate as ever about spaceships. He has built 724 classic models since helping to save the world. Though he still hasn't fixed his broken space helmet.

WE ARE ALL SPECIAL!

Having saved the world, Emmet now enjoys evenings at home watching TV with his friends on his double-decker couch. He hopes not to be called on to save the world again any time soon...

EMMET

Unikitty continues the battle to keep the angrier side of her nature at bay. It's much easier now that Lord Business has stopped making up so many silly rules.

WORLD

THERE'S NOTHING MORE SPECIAL THAN MY OUTFIT!

I'M STILL MORE SPECIAL THAN MOST PEOPLE.

Lord Business is no longer pursuing his plans to control the world, but he still likes to wear his almighty elevated suit at every opportunity.

With his newfound teamwork skills, Batman is thinking of teaming up with Superman, Green Lantern, Wonder Woman and other heroes. He is also writing deep and meaningful music on his feelings about his lost love, Wyldstyle.

MetalBeard still sails the seven seas. He tells anyone who will listen about the dramatic day he helped save the world. He swears he recognised Emmet's potential before anyone else did.

Wyldstyle isn't so worried about being cool anymore. She now goes by her real name, Lucy. No longer in a relationship with Batman, Lucy will probably be spending more time with a 'Special' person in her life.

His legendary made-up prophecy changed the world. To this day, Ghost Vitruvius continues to advise his fellow Master Builders in spirit.

BEHIND THE SCENES

Matthew Ashton is Vice President of Design for Playthemes and Intellectual Properties at the LEGO Group. He is also an Executive Producer on *The LEGO® Movie*, and the creator of Unikitty. DK asked Matthew how *The LEGO Movie* came to life.

What inspired the look of *The LEGO Movie*?

The directors were inspired by the visual style of the stop-motion videos created by our fan community, which can be found online. However, a feature-length stop-motion movie would take years and years to develop, and there probably wouldn't have been enough bricks on the entire planet (in the right colours) to get it done! So the stop-motion videos were used as a starting point, and we then imagined what kind of universe, characters and story could be created in the same style with an infinite number of LEGO bricks. The final movie animation was then created digitally, but made to look as close to traditional stop-motion animation as possible.

Matthew is based at the LEGO Group headquarters in Billund, Denmark.

Design Master Gitte Thorsen sculpts Vitruvius's wig, a LEGO piece that was created specifically for *The LEGO Movie*.

How did the animations develop?

LEGO sculpting designers created new pieces for the movie, developing them in the same way they would for a real LEGO toy. Every component in the movie is a digital 3-D representation of a real LEGO brick; from the characters, buildings and locations to the visual effects, like bubbling lava, ocean waves and plumes of smoke! To achieve a realistic effect, the LEGO Group shipped bricks to the animation studio, Animal Logic. The studio looked at the pieces under a magnifying glass, and then resurfaced the digital files to make them look more authentic. If you look closely at the minifigure characters, you can see scratches, teeth-marks and fingerprints. Emmet even has grime in his leg holes, and Vitruvius looks like he has tumbled around in a toy box!

How did you choose the LEGO locations?

There were many LEGO worlds and themes that we wanted to explore within *The LEGO Movie,* but they wouldn't all fit! Bricksburg had to be in there. It's where Emmet lives and the story begins, but it is also how many people imagine a LEGO world to be, from playing or building cities with their own LEGO bricks. An Old Western town seemed like a great location for a classic chase sequence. As Lord Business is set on stamping out creativity in the movie, we also needed a location that was the complete opposite to his vision – a world where creativity had no limits, and imaginations could run free – so Cloud Cuckoo Land was created for the movie as a colourful, creative, magical land where there are no rules.

How did you develop the main characters?

They developed along with the story. As the story is very much centred around 'building', the obvious job to give the main character, Emmet, was that of a construction worker. Wyldstyle was then created to be everything that Emmet wasn't: bold, confident, slick and streetwise, with mind-blowing building skills! We also couldn't make a LEGO movie without an iconic LEGO spaceman, complete with worn-away logo. A crack was added to Benny's LEGO helmet, since this was a common flaw with these helmets when they were first made. We worked extremely hard on MetalBeard, loading him up with every LEGO pirate ship icon we could think of, while making sure his size and movement were right for animation. Unikitty was the last of the gang to be created – we wanted her to be almost entirely brick-built to reflect her creativity.

Matthew and Michael Fuller work hard to keep track of the many minifigure characters in the movie.

Michael looks over some of the models he hand-built, including MetalBeard and Emmet's mech.

How much of *The LEGO Movie* set was developed as real LEGO models?

Our focus from a LEGO perspective was to be highly involved in the development of the most prominent models seen in the movie, so we worked closely with the directors and animators to develop them as real models. The animation team was then entirely responsible for digitally creating all of the landscapes, crowds, buildings and background vehicles, based on the directors' briefings and taking inspiration from existing LEGO sets and artwork. Sometimes the directors had a very clear idea of what they wanted a key model to look like, and other times they came to the LEGO team for suggestions. Michael Fuller, Senior Product Designer at the LEGO Group, hand-built many of the key models from scratch. He had weekly video conferences with the film-makers, where amendments were suggested until the final LEGO model was realised. Some models, like Bad Cop's flying cop car, flew through the development process, while others, like MetalBeard, took a lot of refining!

Matthew and Concept Designer Matteo Oliverio finalise Unikitty's adorable design.

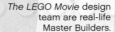

The LEGO Movie design team are real-life Master Builders.

LONDON, NEW YORK, MUNICH,
MELBOURNE AND DELHI

Senior Editor Hannah Dolan
Senior Designer Nathan Martin
Editorial Assistant Beth Davies
Managing Editor Elizabeth Dowsett
Design Manager Ron Stobbart
Publishing Manager Julie Ferris
Art Director Lisa Lanzarini
Publishing Director Simon Beecroft
Pre-Production Producer Siu Yin Chan
Producer Louise Daly

The LEGO© Movie screenplay by
Phil Lord and Christopher Miller

The LEGO© Movie story by
Dan Hageman & Kevin Hageman
and Phil Lord & Christopher Miller

Dorling Kindersley would like to thank Randi Sørensen and Matthew James Ashton at the LEGO
Group; and Jo Casey and Richard Horsford at DK for editorial and design assistance.

First published in Great Britain in 2014 by
Dorling Kindersley Limited
80 Strand, London WC2R 0RL
A Penguin Random House Company

10 9 8 7 6 5 4 3 2 1

001–193694–Jan/14

Colour reproduction in the UK by Altaimage
Printed and bound by TBB, a.s., Slovakia

**Discover more at
www.dk.com
www.LEGO.com**